Part I: Silence in Pr.

Silence shall always be regarded as one of the chief privileges of the Community, for it prepares the way for the union of the soul with the will of God and is an offering of perpetual reverence to his majesty. It is in silence that the spirit will be trained to deepen recollection and to exercise itself after the likeness of the Seraphim and Cherubim that worship round the throne of God. But it should be remembered that silence must cover all the levels of the conscious life; there must be an outward silence of speech and movement, a silence of the mind for the overcoming of vain imaginations and distractions, and a silence of the soul in the surrender of the will to be still and know that God is God, leading to a silence of spirit which is the preparation for the fulness of contemplation.

That passage comes from the chapter on silence in our *Rule of the Sisters of the Love of God*. It is a key passage, not only in that particular chapter but in the Rule as a whole, and it is because of it, in a sense, that you have come here today—that you might for a few hours taste the quality of a life which regards silence as one of its chief privileges, and so return refreshed, one hopes, to the natural clamour of a world which cannot be organized with silence as its keystone to the same extent. Nevertheless, properly understood, silence belongs as much to your life as priests as it does to ours as religious, and in these two addresses we will think together in what ways that claim may be realised, in this first one by considering the question of silence in prayer and in the second the question of silence in action, regarding prayer and action as distinct, like the Persons of the Trinity, but, so to speak, one in being, that is, united by the silence from which both true prayer and true action proceed.

But before we consider silence in prayer we might first question the whole notion of the desirability of silence. What is so good about it? you may ask. Why do we regard silence as one of the chief privileges of our Community? Is it really the preparation for the union of the soul with the will of God? Are there not thousands, even millions, of Christians living in the light of the Gospel whose lives altogether lack silence and who know nothing of the practice of silence in prayer? Yes, very probably. But whatever may or may not be true of others will stand us in no stead on that Great Day when we are required to answer for every idle word! It is not possible to judge our fellow-Christians on this question, but I think we may say that where silence in prayer is not being practised something vital to the Christian life is not being developed. Let me put it like this.

In every Christian life there should be a two or three-fold development of the Holy Spirit's work through baptism and these developments could be seen in terms of distinct calls: the 'common', the 'particular' and the 'unique'. The 'common' call begins at baptism and grows, through grace, until we are drawn to make a conscious decision to live in accordance with our baptismal vows. This 'common' call is all-embracing; it cannot be superseded in any sense; there is nothing 'higher'. Our Rule recognises this in its opening paragraph: 'All Christians are called through baptism to sanctification in a life of total commitment to the service of God' (Ch. 1 'The Monastic State'). However within this 'common' call, sanctification in a life of total commitment will require for some Christians a response to the 'particular'—the call to the priesthood or the religious life, for instance. But for all Christians there is the 'unique' call, that is, the call to develop a unique relationship with the God who made each one of us in his image and likeness, and on whom, in this 'unique' stage, we become wholly dependent and thus uniquely and wonderfully ourselves, filling a place in relation to both God and to our fellow-creatures which only we and none other can fill. This secret and ultimate vocation to realise our uniqueness can only, I believe, be developed in silence before God. It is here we are given a foretaste of that final fulfilment expressed by the Psalmist: 'When I awake up after thy likeness I shall be satisfied with it' (Ps. 17:16).

This, then, is what is so good about silence, for it is in silence that we come to ourselves and arise for the return journey to our heavenly home. We see, moreover, in the terms I am using, that the 'common' and the 'unique' calls are the essential ones. And this is important to understand for what can happen, wherever religion is structured to provide places for the 'particular', is that the 'common' Christian who has not been called to the particular can be held back from entering the unique by the assumption that the particular call, far from being merely intermediary, is the ultimate and therefore superior one. When those called to the particular themselves believe this they are liable to fall under our Lord's condemnation: 'Woe to you scribes and pharisees, hypocrites! For ye shut up the kingdom of heaven against men: for ye neither go in yourselves, neither suffer ye them that are entering to go in' (Matt. 23:13). But, wherever the blame lies, the 'common' Christian who is not going into the kingdom, that is, who is not entering the unique, will either settle down into the structure—sadly or smugly, according to temperament (and any PCC provides rich material for the study of the 'common' Christian—the self-deprecating sidesman, for instance, who claims to be just a simple bloke, not like the Vicar—and so on); or they will react against the particular call and either ignore the structure which provides for it (and go off to India, perhaps) or become belligerent about it, and even try in some way or other to muscle in on it.

Likewise the person who has responded to the particular call can come to feel equally shut out of the kingdom if he does not understand that there is more to his life than being, for instance, a priest. He can become stuck in his role, and if that happens he will be prone to frustrations and excessive sensitivity to the seeming fatuities of his ecclesiastical superiors—who may also be stuck in the particular—or be over-confident in his interpretation of his priestly ministry and, by assuming authority for himself, fail to mediate the authority of the One he is serving.

These are dangers which attend the particular call if we think, in responding to it, that we have 'done all'. No we are still unprofitable servants; we have only done that which was our duty to do (cf. Luke 17:10). There remains our unique call to answer. But we answer it not in order to be taken beyond the particular—rather the contrary. We answer it the better to be able to fulfil the particular. I know—and I am sure you know the same for

3

yourselves—that if I were to abandon my particular call the pursuit of the unique would be sheer illusion. So it is right for us to be identified with our particular call. A deeply moving example of this right identification was the simple response, 'I am a priest', to the question, 'Who are you?' when Maximilian Kolbe stepped forward to offer himself for the death cell in place of another prisoner. He might have said, 'I am Maximilian Kolbe', or 'I am a Franciscan friar', or even, to his German interrogator, 'I am a Pole'. But in that moment everything both common and unique in him was wholly concentrated in the particular—his priesthood. And so the sacrifice of his life became the consummation of his priestly ministry; and by his sacrifice he ministered throughout that terrible week not only to his fellow-condemned but to the whole camp. And he continues, in the communion of saints, to mediate his priesthood by his confession of it in the face of death.

And so now, the better to fulfil our particular call, we turn to consider the unique—that which I have suggested can only be developed in silence. Let us start by diving into the deep end with a long extract from a letter on prayer by John the Solitary, a Syrian monk who lived, it is thought, in the fifth century:

Do not imagine, brother, that prayer consists solely of words, or that it can be learnt by means of words. No, the truth of the matter, you should understand, is that spiritual prayer does not reach fulness as a result of either learning or the repetition of words. For it is not to a man that you are praying, before whom you can repeat a well-composed speech; it is to Him who is Spirit that you are directing the movements of your prayer. You should pray therefore in spirit, seeing that He is Spirit.

No special place is required for someone who prays in fulness to God. Our Lord said, 'The hour is coming when you will not be worshipping the Father in this mountain or in Jerusalem'; and again, to show that no special place was required, he also taught that those who worship the Father should 'worship Him in spirit and in truth'; and in the course of his instructing us why we should pray thus he said, 'For God is a Spirit', and He should be praised spiritually, in the spirit. Paul too tells us about this spiritual prayer and psalmody which we should employ: 'What then shall I do?', he says, 'I will pray in spirit and pray in my mind; I will sing in the spirit and I will sing in my mind'. It is in spirit and in mind, then, that he says one should pray and sing to God; he does not say anything at all about the tongue. The reason is that this spiritual prayer is more interior than the tongue, more deeply interiorized than anything on the lips, more interiorized than any words or vocal song. When someone prays this kind of prayer he has sunk deeper than all speech, and he stands where spiritual beings and angels are to be found; like them he utters 'holy' without any words . . .

For God is silence, and in silence is He sung by means of that psalmody which is worthy of Him. I am not speaking of the silence of the tongue, for if someone merely keeps his tongue silent, without knowing how to sing in mind and spirit, then he is simply unoccupied and becomes filled with evil thoughts; he is just keeping an exterior silence and he does not know how to sing in an interior way, seeing that the tongue of his 'hidden man' has not yet learnt to stretch itself out even to babble. You should look on the spiritual infant that is within you in the same way as you do on an ordinary child or infant; just as the tongue placed in an infant's mouth is still because it does not yet know speech or the right movements for speaking, so it is with that interior tongue of the mind; it will be still from all speech and from all thought; it will simply be placed there, ready to learn the first babblings of spiritual utterance.

Thus there is a silence of the tongue, there is a silence of the whole body, there is the silence of the soul, there is the silence of the mind, and there is the silence of the spirit. The silence of the tongue is merely when it is not incited to evil speech; the silence of the entire body is when all its senses are unoccupied; the silence of the soul is when there are not ugly thoughts bursting forth within it; the silence of the mind is when it is not reflecting on any harmful knowledge or wisdom; the silence of the spirit is when the mind ceases even from stirrings caused by created spiritual beings and all its movements are stirred solely by Being, at the wondrous awe

5

of the silence which surrounds Being.

These are the degrees and measures to be found in speech and silence. But if you have not reached these and find yourself still far away from them, remain where you are and sing to God using the voice and the tongue in love and awe. Stand in awe of God, as is only right, and you will thus be held worthy to love Him with a pure love—Him who was given to us at our renewal [baptism] . . .

From 'John the Solitary, *On Prayer*'*

That is all very simple—yet it is very difficult too, and in order to expand some of its points I shall use another substantial extract from the Eastern tradition, this time nearer home and by one of our contemporaries, Kallistos Ware, from a paper he wrote called 'Silence in Prayer: The Meaning of Hesychia'. The full sense of this word *hesychia* unfolds during the course of the paper, but in principle, Father Kallistos explains, it is a general term for inward prayer, and a hesychast is one who practises such prayer, while hesychasm, of course, refers to the prayer itself. The following extract begins at the section entitled 'Hesychia and Spiritual Poverty':

Inward stillness, when interpreted as a guarding of the heart and a return into oneself, implies a passage from multiplicity to unity, from diversity to simplicity and spiritual poverty. To use the terminology of Evagrius, the mind must become 'naked'. This aspect of *hesychia* is made explicit in another definition provided by St John Climacus: '*Hesychia* is a laying aside of thoughts'. Here he is adapting an Evagrian phrase, 'Prayer is a laying aside of thoughts'. *Hesychia* involves a progressive self-emptying, in which the mind is stripped of all visual images and man-made concepts, and so contemplates in purity the realm of God . . .

This 'pure silence', although it is termed 'spiritual poverty', is far from being a mere absence or privation. If the hesychast strips his mind of all man-made concepts, so far as this is possible, his aim in this 'self-noughting' is altogether constructive—that he may be filled with an all-embracing sense of the

*Translated by Sebastian Brock in the *Journal of Theological Studies*, April 1979, pp. 97-99.

Divine indwelling. The point is well made by St Gregory of Sinai: 'Why speak at length? Prayer is God, who works all things in men'. Prayer is God; it is not primarily something which I do but something which God is doing in me—'not I, but Christ in me'. The hesychast programme is exactly delineated in the words of the Baptist concerning the Messiah: 'He must increase, but I must decrease'. The hesychast ceases from his own activity, not in order to be idle, but in order to enter into the activity of God. His silence is not vacant and negative—a blank pause between words, a short rest before resuming speech—but intensely positive: an attitude of alert attentiveness, of vigilance, and above all of *listening*.

The hesychast is *par excellence* the one who *listens*, who is open to the presence of Another: 'Be still and know that I am God' . . . Returning into himself, the hesychast enters the secret chamber of his own heart in order that, standing there before God, he may listen to the wordless speech of his Creator. 'When you pray', observes a contemporary Orthodox writer in Finland, 'you yourself must be silent; let the prayer speak'—more exactly, let God speak . . . Understood in these terms, as an entering into the life and the activity of God, *hesychia* is something which during this present age men can achieve only to a limited and imperfect degree. It is an eschatological reality, reserved in its fulness for the Age to Come. In the words of St Isaac: 'Silence is a symbol of the future world'.

Op. cit., published in *One Yet Two**

In those two extracts from John the Solitary and Kallistos Ware we are told *what* to do and *why* we should do it—that we should lay aside all thoughts so that we may listen in silence to God's wordless voice speaking within us, becoming passive to him that he might be active in us. But there is more to be said on *how* we should do it and on what actually happens when we attempt to attain silence in prayer.

First of all, one of the paradoxes of pure prayer is that we suppose we shall become aware only of God but find, in the

*Papers of the Orthodox-Cistercian Symposium, Oxford 1973, Cistercian Publications, 1976, pp.30-33.

laying aside of thoughts, that we become aware instead of our own body. This is wholly right. It is now we discover the perfect unity which exists between body, mind and spirit, and that the least lack of surrender in any of these parts is at once reflected in all of them. It is indeed something of a hen-and-egg question as to which comes first: tensions in the body producing tensions in the mind and spirit, or tensions in the mind or spirit producing tensions in the body. Until the last few years the problem of how to dispose the body in prayer so that it may be as free from tensions as possible has not been much discussed in the Western Christian tradition. But with the penetration of Oriental ideas some welcome light has been shed on it, and in one of our publications, *Prayer and Contemplation*, Robert Llewelyn, a priest who has spent several years in India, gives some helpful instructions, as the following extract will, I think, show:

The basic requirement in posture is that the back should be held straight in an easy tension. This applies in whatever position we adopt—whether we stand, sit or kneel upright; or kneel sitting on the heels, perhaps with the help of a cushion or prayer stool . . . The rule should be to adopt whatever position we can maintain without undue strain. Let us assume we have chosen to sit on an upright chair. Holding the back straight in an easy tension will assist a natural counter-relaxation of the temples and forehead, and the muscles of the face and jaw. The mouth should be shut, but not tightly so; the eyes closed and relaxed . . . the hands resting palms downwards on the upper part of the thighs, or palms upwards in the lap. The classic position for the head is erect, firmly set on the neck, the back, neck and head forming one straight line . . . I believe there is value in knowing and saying these things but I would not wish to be over-assertive about them. I have great respect for the approach of *The Cloud of Unknowing*, which is to lay down no rules but simply allow the body to straighten out naturally to its correct position as the prayer proceeds. Yet I am sure there is need for this other approach as well, and it must be left to the individual to find the right balance between the two.

Op. cit., Revised Edition 1980, p. 53.

The right balance comes, I think, when both approaches are used simultaneously; when in the moment of, say, sitting down to pray, we drop everything in our head while consciously relaxing from the feet upwards. If we then say with our whole being, 'Into thy hands, O Lord, I commend my spirit', whatever happens after that belongs, however unlikely it may seem, to our deepening relationship with God, to the secret converse of our soul with our Maker.

And it is secret converse—secret even from ourselves. Precisely because God is silence, as John the Solitary says, it is not possible for us, who know only how to interpret sounds, to have much more idea of what is going on behind our screen of monkey-chatter, which continues at the ordinary level of consciousness, than anyone else; nor can we understand why, if the chatter should be blessedly suspended, the light doze we may fall into is more refreshing than several hours' sleep—though it has truly been, in Father Gilbert Shaw's lovely phrase, 'a resting in the love of God'. But while our mind remains restless in a multiplicity of thoughts, it is desirable to keep presenting it with a single counter-thought. I quote again from the paper by Kallistos Ware:

> It is surely evident to each one of us that we cannot halt the inward flow of images and thoughts by a crude exertion of will-power. It is of little or no value to say to ourselves, 'Stop thinking'; we might as well say, 'Stop breathing'. 'The rational mind cannot rest idle', insists St Mark the Monk. How then are we to achieve spiritual poverty and inner silence? Although we cannot make the never-idle intelligence desist altogether from its restlessness, what we can do is to simplify and unify its activity by continually repeating a short formula of prayer. The flow of images and thoughts will persist, but we shall be enabled gradually to detach ourselves from it. The repeated invocation will help us to 'let go' the thought presented to us by our conscious or subconscious self. This 'letting go' seems to correspond to what Evagrius had in view when he spoke of prayer as a 'laying aside of thoughts'—not a savage conflict, not a ruthless campaign of furious aggression, but a gentle yet persistent act of detachment. (p. 35).

'By their fruits shall ye know them.' Yes, indeed. But let us think not of our fruits (we cannot be sure about *our* fruits until we are safely dead!) but of the fruits of those who have gone before, of, for instance, a man who was above all a great priest, St Francis de Sales, and who had this to say on our subject: 'If you spend half an hour gently returning your mind to God, you will have spent the time very well.'

Part II: Silence in Action

If we want to understand silence in prayer we must look to the kingdom within, to the indwelling Christ. If we want to understand silence in action we must look at the Lord of the Gospels, at the Incarnate Christ who 'secretly, in the midst of the silence . . . leapt down from his royal throne', and from that amazing moment continued to speak his all-powerful words from the midst of the silence until the final return and the last words, spoken from the all-embracing silence of the cross: 'Into thy hands I commend my spirit.'

In Jesus we see a perfect balance between inner silence and outer activity; in him we see silence in activity and activity in silence. It is to this balance and this permeation of one with the other that we aspire and to the gaining of which our lives should be directed. Apart from our times of silent prayer, the means *par excellence* is the Divine Office which halts our activity and returns us at regular intervals to the well-springs of silence. This alternation between activity and the silence of the Psalter enables us to become, in the words of Max Picard, 'anchored to eternal silence as a ship is anchored to the sea-bed'.

Then [he goes on], whenever a man begins to speak, the word comes from silence at each new beginning. The man whose nature is . . . possessed by silence moves out from the silence into the outside world. The silence is central in the man. In the world of silence movement is not directly from one man to another but from the silence in one man to the silence in the other . . . A man in whom the substance of silence is . . . an active force carries the silence into every movement. His movements, therefore, do not jolt violently against each other; they are borne by the silence; they are simply the waves of silence.

Quoted by Paul Maréchal in *Cistercian Studies* 1973:3

'The silence is central in the man.' The Gospels speak of the silence of Jesus in every incident. They convey vividly the impression that, whenever he begins to speak, the word 'comes from silence at each new beginning'. We can *hear* the silence before he says, 'Simon, I have somewhat to say to thee'; we can both hear and see his silent gaze at a man before he says, 'follow me', or 'thy faith hath made thee whole'. The *active* power of Jesus' silence is astonishing. But there is another side to it, the *passive* power, which is even more astonishing. Consider his silence when the woman 'which was a sinner . . . stood at his feet behind him weeping, and began to wash his feet with tears and wipe them with the hairs of her head, and kissed them, and anointed them with ointment' (Luke 7:37-38). The attention in this story naturally focusses on the woman and what she is *doing* so that we are liable to miss the significance of Jesus' part and what he is *being*. But imagine yourself in Jesus' place for a moment! A disreputable woman, kissing your feet, and at a respectable dinner-party too! The very thought is enough to make a man blush deep purple and to set up an inner chatter so deafening that nothing else would stand much chance of being heard!

'Why do thoughts arise in your hearts?' Jesus asked his disciples when he appeared to them after his resurrection—a question of immense significance, I think, for it indicates the measure of inner silence and tranquillity he requires of them in the face of the unexpected, even in the face of an apparition, as they then thought. And his expectations would hardly be less in a situation like the one with the weeping woman.

A priest celebrating the Eucharist is, it seems to me, the perfect 'icon' of silence in action. So, also, the picture of the Lord having his feet washed with tears provides another icon for silence in action. But in the first we see the active side of silence in action, and in all such works as celebrating, preaching, and evangelisation of any kind, the role of the priest to mediate the

11

active Christ is easily understood. In the second we are given a model for the mediation of the passive Christ—and this is much less easily understood. How should we understand it?

In the story of the woman at Jesus' feet we are clearly presented with a further stage of his ministry to her. He has, we may assume, already *acted* in relation to her, either by casting out the seven devils of another account, or by liberating her with the command, 'Go, and sin no more', or in some other way. But whatever it was, it was only one half of the complete cure. His ministry to her must continue if what has been begun in her is not to be spoiled and stunted, and what is now required of him is that he be *passive* in relation to her, that he receive in simplicity and stillness the consequences of the effect he has had on her. And, of course, being who he is, he is able to. May you be spared from ever having so much required!

Yet, in less dramatic forms, the priest is constantly being required to be passive as a consequence of having been effectively active. He may, for instance, preach a sermon which pierces the heart of a member of his congregation. But then he may fail in the moment of being thanked for it. We do, alas, find it difficult to be praised, especially if our own parents and teachers have taken the line that praise only leads to swelled heads so that we grow up quite unfitted to receive it naturally. But souls are at stake and God is at work, and self-consciousness is inappropriate.

However, it is not only self-consciousness which prevents the exercise of the passive side of ministry. There is always the fear, when faced with a reaction which threatens to overstep conventionally-accepted limits, 'Where is this going to lead?' I once heard a wise man asked the question: 'How does one avoid getting involved with people?' and the answer came back immediately: 'Give them your full attention.' I repeated this later to a priest. After a moment's thought he agreed and, by way of illustration, told me that some time earlier one of his parishioners had taken it into her head to fall in love with him. 'Me!' he exclaimed, pointing at himself with a modesty which, it must be admitted, was not entirely unjustified. But, being a man of sense, he took her out to lunch and said: 'Now look here, this nonsense has got to stop'—and it did, immediately!

An hour or so of full attention effected a complete cure. A quite different story but, again, an example of the healing power of full attention, this time accompanied by actual silence as well, was that of a hospital matron to whom it fell to break the news to a young man, newly-married, that his wife had just died. She did not tell him but simply took him to her office and sat with him, neither speaking a word. After twenty minutes or so he rose to his feet. 'Thank you', he said, 'I have never felt so consoled in my life.'

That matron was an exceptional person, but I am sure one of the reasons for the power of the medical profession at the present time, and for the queues of patients both in hospitals and the waiting-rooms of any GP, is that by and large doctors, perhaps due to the system within which they work, are not afraid to give their full attention, however briefly, to their patients. The tendency, on the other hand, among those who undertake the priestly role to fail in this respect is noted by Jesus in the Parable of the Good Samaritan. If we take it that a *soul* is being talked about and not a body the story becomes not only comprehensible but of daily occurrence. The priest and the levite looked but they did not *see* a soul stripped and wounded and half dead. Perhaps what they did see was an aggressive man, irritatingly over-opinionated; or an attractive woman, too sophisticated to embarrass a poor clergyman with the wounds life had inflicted on her. In any case, whatever kind of person they saw it was not a kind which, to their unpenetrating gaze, stood in need of help. But thank heaven for many signs that these things are being better understood and that the clergy are immeasurably more open to all sorts and conditions of men than they were, say, even ten years ago.

In Matthew, chapter five, there is a little collection of four very hard sayings indeed (vv. 38-42), all of which are answers to the question, 'How does one avoid getting involved with people?' and the one which says, in effect, give them your full attention' is: 'Whosoever shall compel thee to go a mile, go with him twain.' But all four are directives concerning the passive aspect of ministry: 'Resist not evil, but whosoever shall smite thee on thy right cheek, turn to him the other also. And if any man sue thee at law, and take away thy coat, let him have thy cloke also . . . Give to him that asketh thee, and from him that would borrow of thee, turn not thou away.' Hard sayings; but what is hard about them is the *thought* of them. The actual practice turns out to be not only surprisingly easy but has results which are precisely contrary to those we expect, sending our smiter or borrower happily on his way, released from his needs in relation to us. Such experiences delight and refresh the soul and yet remain elusive because knowledge—even knowledge gained from experience—is never enough. What is always necessary is to remain 'anchored to eternal silence as a ship is anchored to the sea-bed'. For the essence of full attention is inner silence. Without inner silence the passive side of ministry cannot be developed; and if it is not developed we will always be too busy, too entangled in situations, to develop ourselves and so be able to help others in their development.

We have been reading together here recently a very wonderful book, *Community and Growth*, by Jean Vanier, the founder of the L'Arche communities for mentally handicapped people, and from a chapter called 'Welcome' come the following three passages which are closely connected with our subject:

> Sometimes when people knock at my door I ask them in and we talk, but I make it clear to them in a thousand small ways that I am busy, that I have other things to do. The door of my office is open, but the door of my heart is closed. I still have a lot to learn and a long way to go. When we welcome people, we open the door of our heart to them and give them space within it. And if we have other things to do which really can't wait, we should say so—but open our heart all the same.   (p. 195)

> It is always a risk to welcome anyone. It is always disturbing. But did not Jesus come precisely to disturb our routines, comforts and apathy? We need constant stimulation if we are not to become dependent on security and comfort, if we are to continue to progress from the slavery of sin and egoism towards the promised land of liberation.

> To welcome is not primarily to open the doors of our house. It is to open the doors of our hearts and become vulnerable. It is a spirit, an inner attitude. It means accepting the other

14

into ourselves, even if this means insecurity. It is to be concerned for others, attentive towards them, and to help them find their place in the Community or in life itself. To welcome means even more than to listen. (p.197)

The first welcome is very often the important one. People can flee because it has put them off. Others stay because of a smile or an initial act of kindness. People should not be made to feel that they are upsetting things when they arrive. They should be able to feel that we are happy to share with them. We have to know how to respond sympathetically to a letter or a phone call, how to add a personal note of gratuity. If we really welcome each new person as a gift of God, and as His messenger, we will be more loving and open. (p.199)

You will notice, however, that Jean Vanier in those passages is not quite making the point I think Jesus is making in the saying: 'Whosoever shall compel thee to go a mile, go with him twain.' Jean Vanier is concerned with what we are doing to the other; Jesus, it seems to me, is here concerned first with what we are doing to ourselves. He wants us to be free of other people so that we can be free for God, free to pray, to intercede, to praise, to stand in silence before him, to grow in our relationship with him. And in order to be free of others we must give them *more* not less than they ask for. There is a tough realism rooted in a spiritual law in these four sayings which it is hard for us to grasp because our idea of what Christianity is about tends to be shot through with sentimentality. And sentimentality is the enemy of true compassion and effective action.

The passive aspect of ministry, then, is the other and too often neglected side of the active aspect. Both are equally important; both depend for their value on the quality, so to speak, of the metal in which they are cast. The concluding paragraph of our Rule gives a directive which, although addressed to a monastic community, has an application for every Christian:

While the spirit of silence serves to separate each individual life unto God, the spirit of love must ever be binding all together in God, that in the unity of the Spirit all may seek their perfection by holy charity.

By the Same Author

PRAYER THE WORK OF THE SPIRIT

How can we pray when there seems to be no end to the other important things clamouring for our attention—and why should we? In this talk, given originally to a group of young mothers who visited the convent to learn about prayer, Sister Edmée insists on the first step: stop—and decide that now, for however short a time, prayer is the most important thing; and ultimately the most helpful.

Having acted on that conviction we may find that a further difficult surrender to God is required of us, for even in our well-meaning efforts to pray we may be trying to do too much ourselves. Instead, we are being asked, like the Mother of Jesus, to open ourselves to God's activity in us, to the work of the Spirit.

Fairacres Publication 93
Price 75 pence

ISBN 0 7283 0106 7
ISSN 0307-1405